Ernie J. Zelinski

Life's Secret Handbook

Reminders for Adventurous Souls Who Want to Make a Big Difference in This World

Copyright © 2017 by Ernie J. Zelinski

All rights reserved, including the right to reproduce this work in any form whatsoever, without permission in writing from the publisher, except for brief passages in connection with a review.

Direct any inquiries about foreign rights and quantity purchases to:
Ernie Zelinski
Visions International Publishing
P.O. Box 4072
Edmonton, Alberta, Canada, T6E 4S8
Phone (780) 434-9202
E-mail: vip-books@telus.net

ISBN: 978-0-9813118-3-8
Printed in South Korea

Dedication

This complete creative work is dedicated to my special and long time friend Forrest Bard who passed away suddenly in September 2017. I had promised Forrest the first print copy of this handbook but he moved on to another dimension before I could give it to him. Forrest, you meant so much to your friends, your relatives, and me. We all miss you dearly.

To whoever winds up with this handbook: You are privileged to own one copy of only 500 printed; billions on this planet do not own one. It is no accident that this handbook has found its way to you. Your duty is to put it to good use. Open this handbook at random and reflect on the content. Perhaps the words on the page you arrive at will be of life-changing significance to you. Please share what you learn with others.

— Traveling Monk from the Himalayas

(This passage appeared in the inspirational fable *Look Ma, Life's Easy* from which *Life's Secret Handbook* evolved.)

1
Life's Secret Handbook

Every great accomplishment in the history of humanity started with one small thought.

We all have these thoughts.

Few people do anything with theirs, however.

What do you intend to do with yours?

Search, above all, for dreams worth pursuing.

Having found these dreams, dare to pursue them with all your heart and soul.

It is a mistake not to.

The regret of unfulfilled dreams is the most sorrow you will ever experience.

To be open to the great rewards that the Universe wants to bestow on you, you must have an idea or a dream or a passion.

And you must act on it.

You must turn the inspiration within into powerful, purposeful action.

You must resonate in body, mind, and spirit — and vibrate with the kind of imagination, frequency, and creativity that transcends ordinary human behavior.

Being successful and happy in this world is not as hard as you believe.

Keep these two generally unknown truths in mind:

What appear to be the easiest things in life are often the most difficult;

And what appear to be the most difficult are much easier than most people ever imagine.

Imagine that you are in control of your life.

Now, the question is:

Why do you have to imagine this?

You aren't here on Earth simply to earn a decent living.

The more you forget about your true mission, the more senseless living becomes.

You are here to bring hope and enrichment for others so that they too are inspired to greater heights with your vision of a better world.

Have you forgotten this mission?

The rest of the world will be shortchanged if you do not pursue it.

Life is a game.

Happy people are the players.

Unhappy people are the spectators.

Which would you like to be?

~

You have dedicated the years you have lived on Earth so far to become the person that you are today.

Has it been worth it?

At the foundation of everyone's life – including yours – is one central desire:

Wanting to know that one's life matters, that there is some important meaning to it.

~

When you learn how to be in tune with your true spirit and start doing the adventurous things that the majority is not doing, you will start creating what the majority calls "miracles."

There is within you a second self,
an unlived and unsatisfied soul.

Listen to the soft voice within.

It's telling you everything you
need to know about who you
want to become — and can!

~

Do not embrace what you don't
want.

You are liable to get it.

Avoid tuning into frequencies
that focus your thoughts on the
things that irritate or upset you.

The reality from which you
are trying to escape should be
the reality that you give least
attention to.

Tune into frequencies that
support your wildest dreams,
the things that you want more
than anything else in this world.

~

Making a big difference in this
world is not dependent on the
conditions in your life.

This is solely dependent on the
temperament of your soul.

Much of the difference you make tomorrow will start with what you do today.

The question is:

What seeds of accomplishment do you intend to plant before the end of the day?

~

The biggest barrier stopping you from getting what you want in life is what you tell yourself about why you can't have what you want.

Being a victim can become a full-time occupation if you are not careful.

That's a horrible way to spend a month or two of your life – not to mention a whole lifetime.

Unfortunately, if you intently and persistently focus on what annoys you, that's what you will get – forever.

~

Observe your thoughts with great care.

If they are anything other than compassionate and blissfully supportive of yourself, change them.

Stay weird.

Follow your unconventional, crazy heart.

Speak what is true to you.

Be honest and be authentic.

Yes, this means taking risks.

But the results will surprise you.

~

Taking risks has nothing to do with having a "death wish."

On the contrary!

This has everything to do with having a "life wish."

When you enter that wondrous world ruled by passion, action, and achievement, you will find the adventure, rewards, and prosperity that you have been seeking.

Indeed, you will not ever again want to return to where you came from.

~

Happiness and making a difference go hand in hand.

Why bother living the way you have been living if you are unhappy and have no satisfaction in your life because you are not making a difference?

To grow and learn anything truly valuable that will make a remarkable difference for you, something must be amiss in your life.

You must set aside the safety of your belief system.

That's not so easy, is it?

~

If your life is not working, take a hard look at your beliefs and your behaviors.

The problem is there somewhere.

Do you matter?

Being cool and hip may be the best racket that you can come up with.

How profound and beneficial is it to you, however, if you are cool and hip — but your life has little meaning?

~

When will you truly matter?

You will truly matter when you make a big difference in other people's lives.

How will you know?

They will tell you.

Most people pass on and leave this planet regretting things they haven't done.

The easiest way to become like them is by joining society's chorus instead of singing your own songs.

~

To know that even one other soul has lived happier and more satisfied because you have contributed magically and immensely to his or her life – this is to have made a difference in this world.

If you want a report from the future about how well you will do with your life a few years from now, consult with your past.

The world is continually providing you with instant feedback.

You can either tune in or tune out of what the world is telling you.

If you tune out and at no time make changes, your past is a clear indication of how well your life will turn out in the future.

~

When you learn to let go of the mundane and the ordinary, the extraordinary will start being part of your life.

Way too many people are looking for an easy way to achievement, success, and riches.

There is no easy way for them.

None for you either.

~

Although prosperity can be viewed as a spiritual goal, it's not something that you easily attain just through affirmations and meditation.

It's something that you "magically" earn using your creativity and integrity, while actively pursuing a worthwhile purpose for the betterment of the Universe.

Do not believe what the charlatan "experts" of this world tell you.

They always have their own interests in mind — and not yours.

~

It's an unvirtuous thing many self-proclaimed spiritual and success gurus do, to excite the minds of so many naive souls with affirmations and meditations about how to attain remarkable wealth and prosperity — without mentioning the inspired action and creative risk-taking required to manifest such remarkable wealth and prosperity.

The ultimate purpose of life is not merely to survive.

Neither is it to have an easy and comfortable existence.

The ultimate purpose of life is to be useful, to matter, to make a big difference for humanity, to leave a legacy and inspiration for others, so that they too will have lived with dedication, with compassion, for the betterment of this world.

~

To begin making a difference in this world, make a difference in just one person's life.

Then another's.

Then another's.

And with time, you will have made a difference in many people's lives.

Why bother living a life devoid of accomplishment, success, and prosperity?

Adventurous successful souls create their lives the way that spiders build their webs – just the way they want them.

Worthwhile dreams and inspired action make the difference.

~

No organization – government or otherwise – can take great care of you.

Organizations aren't capable of this – only you are!

You may have held on to your beliefs, your reasonableness, and your victim consciousness for a long time now.

If so, you have not been getting any meaningful results in your life.

That has set you apart from the people who you secretly admire, those who are successful, prosperous, and making the world a better place.

What are you going to do about that?

What if those successful people who you resent are wiser and more perceptual than you?

Instead of always criticizing and complaining, what if for a change you just listen and pay attention to them?

What would be wrong if you learned from them and in the process ended up making a significant difference in this world?

~

No great people are born into this world – only ordinary people who rise to the occasion when faced with a particularly difficult challenge.

They make something remarkable out of it.

Perhaps you have a lot of life energy tied up in your false beliefs about successful people and your grudges against them.

By letting go and detaching yourself from these beliefs and grudges, you get all that life energy back.

You can now use this life energy to create achievement and prosperity in your life – or you can use it to make up even more mischief in your mind.

~

Always think highly of yourself while affirming this to the world, not in loud announcements, however, but in creative and extraordinary accomplishments that benefit humanity.

"So hard, so difficult," we say.

Things aren't difficult because we have tried them and found them to be so.

Things are difficult because we haven't tried them and continue to think that they are.

You yourself must choose how you will make a difference in this world.

When this happens, you will be in a state of awe at how it all came together.

Do not wait for a message from the Universe to make your life matter.

You are the source of all messages from the Universe.

~

You are not here to impress others.

You are here to make a big difference and to make the world a better place.

Be upbeat and your inner resourcefulness will take you to worthwhile destinations even when major obstacles appear.

Your creative essence is a majestic river — a moving, living part of the Universe.

It will find a new path whenever an old one disappears.

~

Venture to be wise.

You do not know everything with clarity.

Some of what you deem to know with clarity is what you think you know.

Living just to get by is not enough.

Just like the butterfly, an adventurous soul needs a varied and enchanting life – green grass and happy skies, freedom to go where it pleases, and joys that await it.

~

It's the gift to give to others.

It's the gift to give to the Universe.

It's the gift to give to yourself.

It's simply the right gift.

The gift of making the world a better place is the ultimate gift of magic that you want to give.

The respective results tell the story.

The world of a normal, reasonable mind has its defined limits.

The world of a creative, adventurous mind is endless, beyond measure.

~

Stand above the crowd even if you have to stand alone.

There is no greater way to gain self-respect as well as the respect of other honorable souls in this world.

Do not be afraid to be different.

Eccentricity is that sound, yet somewhat questionable character trait, valuable in balmy days as well as in those of sorrow, that transcendentally equips us for those unforeseen spectacles in which we all must play a part.

~

Fitting in with everyone else is not the way to make your mark in society.

You will take your first step to making a difference in this world when you learn how to be truly different.

Only by being truly different can you make a big, big difference.

In the game of wanting to be rewarded for making a difference in this world, you ultimately end up with only one of the following:

1. Results.

    or

2. Reasons why you didn't get results.

~

Reasons only help you sound reasonable.

They have nothing to do with manifesting achievement and prosperity in your life.

Talk all you want to talk about your dreams and how you are going to make a difference in this world.

The most elegant words in the world about what you intend to do count nothing compared to a single well-placed action.

~

Have you ever thought, "Why hasn't anyone done something about that?"

Perhaps it's you who should!

When you elevate yourself high enough to see beyond your self-imposed horizons, you will have vision.

You will also start getting meaningful results.

~

Don't believe what your reasonable mind is telling you.

All it knows is limitation.

Learn to play with your creative mind – to get in touch with that greatness of spirit – that allows you to discover the things that you are capable of doing.

You will then see the way to fly, and then to soar high enough to manifest the possibilities that reasonable minds deem impossible.

You can choose to be happy.

Or you can choose to be miserable.

The amount of life energy required for either is about the same.

Choosing the former means you have the spark of life that unites you in spirit with all living things and puts you on the right track to achievement and prosperity.

~

In the middle of the day, when you feel lazy and unmotivated, let this thought be present:

The Palace of Prosperity is reserved for those who take action with their creative ideas and contribute something worthwhile to humanity.

The key to making your dreams come true is to live your life with passion and commitment.

Dream.

Create.

Do.

Accomplish.

Receive.

You can wind up poor in the midst of economic opportunity and prosperity.

Or you can create riches in the midst of economic decline and chaos.

It depends on how you orchestrate your spirit and your soul.

~

If you can't enjoy spending money with the same degree of satisfaction that you experience while earning it, then your prosperity consciousness needs some serious work.

If you persist in attempting to bring successful, adventurous, and prosperous souls down, some part of you will remain down and keep you from soaring as high as you are capable of soaring — which is the level at which successful, adventurous, and prosperous souls soar.

~

You want to be known for your spirit, your creativity, and the difference you make in this world.

To be nimble-witted, spiritually aware, and street-smart is to be abreast of the advanced and magical workings of the Universe.

Just as important as deciding
what you want in life is
deciding what you don't want.

Allow yourself to let go of those
things that don't make you
happy.

Oddly enough, they aren't always
the easiest things to give up.

~

You have two choices in your
pursuit of what's important to
you:

Make bold moves today, knowing
most things won't work out, but
one or two may.

Or make no moves, knowing
nothing will ever work out.

Beliefs are inevitable.

But when you take your beliefs
and claim that they are truth,
you may be in big trouble.

Many beliefs are accidents
waiting to happen.

We are much more betrayed by
our false beliefs about the world
than by all the negative things
that happen in our lives.

~

You may have your personal
reasons to be skeptical.

This doesn't mean that all the
things you don't believe are
false, however.

There is just one problem with the actionless plan for attaining freedom and prosperity.

It won't work!

~

If your belief system has not manifested the lifestyle and prosperity that you would like, isn't it apparent that the way you think and act need to change?

You always have the freedom to change your belief system and your behavior so that you can create a different future than the one that is presently in store for you if you don't change.

The Truth doesn't care what you believe.

If God exists, then God exists.

If God doesn't exist, then God doesn't exist.

What you believe about God is irrelevant.

Your beliefs about God and everything else about the Universe do not determine what is and what isn't.

The Truth remains the Truth, whether you believe it or not.

In the higher order of the Universe your beliefs are rather insignificant.

Reality will remain the way it is regardless of what you believe.

What is ... is.

And what isn't ... isn't.

Do not confuse the two.

Forget about your "feelings" too.

There are over seven billion other people on this planet with their own unique feelings.

What makes yours so special?

They aren't, by the way, in the higher order of the Universe.

The Universe has other things to be concerned with.

You care about what should be.

The Universe cares about what is.

You care about what is good for you.

The Universe cares about what is good for the Universe.

Guess who wins?

If you want to be a winner, be in harmony with the Universe.

Have you ever considered that your perception of reality could be wrong?

If you haven't, this is a sure sign that it is!

~

Be extremely careful with what you perceive as reality.

Any incorrect perception of it is a lie.

This will cause you all sorts of big problems in life.

You are likely to wind up a bystander in an exciting and happening world.

You do not create your own reality.

You create your own interpretation of reality.

There is a difference, unless, of course, you get the interpretation right.

Most people don't.

What makes you think that you have got it right?

~

When your life has no purpose, no direction, no aim, and no meaning, try doing something extraordinarily different for a change.

You can adjust your perception to a different energy level anytime you want.

Whatever your energy level, it will contribute to the results in your life.

Look for the worst in life and you will find it.

Look for the best and you will find it just as easily.

~

If you don't know how to express gratitude, don't be surprised when nothing good ever shows up on your doorstep.

Hate turnips and successful people?

You likely need some mental adjustment — but at least the turnips are happy!

As for successful people, well, they don't really care all that much about what you hate.

Why should they?

~

If you resent successful people, it is apparent that you won't become successful yourself.

How could you?

You would have to become someone who you resent.

The Universe is your
  playground.

Are you watching?

Or are you playing?

Action makes a big, big difference.

~

Making the simple complex
  doesn't take ingenuity.

Making the complex simple, now,
  that's ingenuity!

The mark of your unhappiness is the depth of your belief in how much you are a victim.

Argue for why you are a victim of circumstances, and guess what?

You are one.

You get to be right about it.

The important question is:

Do you want to be right about it or do you want to be happy?

The price of blaming others is the loss of personal responsibility and accountability.

The price of blaming yourself is the loss of the perverse pleasure of being a victim.

Choose one or the other with great care.

~

Don't let weeds – particularly negative friends and acquaintances – grow around your dreams and aspirations.

One alternative is to blame forces of the Universe and others in this world for your financial problems.

Another is to take matters into your own hands and solve not only your own financial problems, but those of others in this world as well.

The first involves making a lot of noise for why you are a victim.

The second entails making a big difference in this world and becoming truly prosperous and free in the process.

~

How easy it is for us to be generous – particularly with using other people's help and money – when it is ourselves who we see as victims.

Being happy in this world is not your right.

It is your duty and responsibility, however.

~

Everyone seems to want to be somewhere they aren't.

Choose to be where you are right now and you will be happier than 90 percent of humankind.

Be unduly mindful of what you
perceive as a happy life.

A happy life isn't the absence of
unhappiness.

Unhappiness will sneak into your
life whether you want it or not.

So will happiness.

What you choose to do with
either is up to you.

~

You will be able to tell when you
have attained true happiness.

Real happiness doesn't cost much.

Unworkable substitutes do.

Gratitude is a powerful force that can change our experience of life instantly.

Be grateful for many things.

Be grateful for your best friends.

Be grateful for your health.

Be grateful for your creativity.

Above all, be grateful to the Universe for the opportunity to play in its playground.

You will experience an enchanted life of inner happiness that escapes people who do not know how to be grateful.

Show the world that you are sufficiently honorable and persevering to make it on your own, without asking anyone else to pay your way in this world.

You will feel so much better for this.

~

Being totally responsible for your life plan is the one and only satisfying path to true happiness, success, prosperity, and freedom.

If you don't design your own life plan, who is going to do it for you?

Someone else?

Problem is – someone else may not have all that much good planned for you!

This world is divided into individuals who talk big about getting things done and those who actually do things in a big way.

Try, if you can, to belong to the latter.

There's far less competition and the payoffs are much greater.

~

Enjoy the process of accomplishment without undue expectations of specific outcomes.

The idea that you need a particular result at a certain time leads to more trouble than it is worth.

Work towards your goals, but let the Universe surprise you with the extraordinary gifts that come your way.

You alone get to decide how much prosperity and personal freedom you experience in life.

To depend on other forces – including friends, relatives, society, government, and chance events – is to be a slave.

To depend wholly on yourself is to be a Master.

So, slave or Master?

It's your call.

~

Avoid blaming other forces for your biggest problems and mistakes.

Otherwise you must also give these same forces full credit for your most cherished successes.

Make no mistake about it.

The degree of your success and happiness will be determined by the company you keep.

Keep good company and you shall become like them.

Keep bad company and the same applies.

~

Learn to be a good judge of character.

Not everyone's company is an improvement over being alone – even when you are badly craving company.

Thank God that life isn't always easy.

Where would your satisfaction come from?

And the boredom would be unbearable.

~

It seems easier to live the comfortable and conventional, to fit in with the majority.

It's when you live the uncomfortable and unconventional, however, that you make the most of your talents, your creativity, and your actions.

That is also when your life starts being fun, satisfying, and meaningful.

Foster a curiosity for the uncommon, regardless of how unpopular it is.

The uncommon is where opportunity likes to hide.

~

Like most people, you undoubtedly have more than one remarkable idea on how to change the world and make it a better place.

Here is a sure way to make the best idea in the Universe totally worthless:

Don't do anything with it!

Anybody can come up with an idea.

This is easy.

But to take an idea and run with it, to do something with it, at the opportune time, for the right purpose, in the right way – is what adventurous, prosperous souls succeed at.

That is not even close to being easy.

~

Be a creator, not only creative.

Everyone is creative, but a true creator actually brings to light something that is useful for humanity and makes a big difference in this world.

As long as excuses are the reason you aren't pursuing your most cherished dreams, your life doesn't belong to you.

You gave it away a long time ago in order to hold on to your most precious excuses and false beliefs.

Whether you get your life back is all up to you.

~

It's all too easy to underestimate yourself as a nuisance in your quest for happiness and peace of mind.

You will likely have more trouble with yourself than anyone else you encounter on this planet.

Do not fall into the trap of being the cowardly soul, the one who always criticizes, but knows neither victory nor defeat.

How easy it is to be critical of successful souls, when you yourself have not accomplished anything important in that particular field, when you do not even know the struggles and failures that successful souls endured on their personal journey to success.

~

Opportunity for making a real difference knocks often.

The question is:

How often are you home?

If your life isn't working, you have problems.

Your problems are not normally ones that someone else created, but ones that you have invited into your life.

~

Think your problems are special and unique?

Not so.

There are only about ten major problems in life.

Everyone has variations of all ten.

So what makes yours so special?

The severity of your problems is
a matter of perspective.

Change your perspective and most
of them become insignificant.

Some of them will no longer exist
as big problems – but enormous
opportunities instead.

~

When your problems no
longer are bigger than you, a
breakthrough occurs.

Your problems no longer matter
all that much.

But your life does.

At this point, making a difference
is a lot easier than you ever
thought possible.

To know, yet to think that you do not know, is putting yourself at a disadvantage.

Not to know, yet to think that you know, is setting yourself up for disaster.

~

Think twice about what you deem as knowledge.

The one thing that the human mind is adept at – more than anything else – is tricking itself into thinking it knows everything about a subject of which it knows very little.

Knowing everything or almost everything is not something to boast about.

There are many worthless things that truly wise people do not bother to know.

~

Knowing more does not mean knowing better.

A grain of knowledge gained that you act on and put to good use is worth a million times more than 10,000 grains of knowledge gained that you don't ever use in bettering this world.

Wisdom begins when you learn to let go of all the things that you know most fiercely and most stubbornly.

~

Regardless of how qualified and deserving you think you are of a much happier and satisfying life, you will not experience it until you have earned it.

You will have to do something remarkable for the rest of the world, something that matters to you too.

Stay away from nasty people and extremely dangerous situations.

All told, it's always easier to stay out of trouble than to get out of trouble.

~

Give serious consideration before lending money to a friend.

You are likely to lose both.

Similarly, be skeptical about lending money to a relative.

A friend or relative who can't get a loan from a bank is a terrible credit risk and likely won't pay you back.

You won't be making a positive difference in this world by lending money to people who don't rightfully pay their debts to others.

When you are experiencing boredom, no doubt you have chosen it.

The question you have to answer is:

Why?

Be careful with your negative thoughts.

They are a thousand times more powerful in contributing to failure and unhappiness than the worst of adversity can ever be.

Adventure may have its risks.

Security and routine, however, can be much more injurious to the soul.

Alter your thoughts and behavior, and you will not only change yourself, but change the world around you.

Whatever psychic energy you put into the Universe will be reflected back at you.

The more positive energy you put into imagining and creating a happy and successful life, the more it will manifest itself in the real world.

~

Open your mind to opinions other than your own.

The people whose opinions you most fear may be the wise ones from whom you can learn most.

Taking full advantage of the present to live the moment and at the same time make a big difference in this world is undeniable proof of your agreement to live your life now – while you have it – and be dead later – when you are.

~

Be certain of this law of the Universe.

Success will elude you as long as you are doing what's wrong for you;

And needless to say, success will come easily when you are doing what's right for you.

Your conscience is a judge of the
integrity of your character.

Listen to it carefully.

And often, too!

~

Great character comes from
maintaining many good habits.

Lousy character comes from
maintaining many bad ones.

Therefore, choose your habits
wisely.

Do not let them choose you.

Character is the basis of success and success is the sanction of character.

Your true character will grow from following your highest sense of spirit, from trusting your creativity, without being totally sure of success.

~

A key test of your character is how you treat people who are down and out and who can't do you any good while your life is working out just the way you want.

If you don't solve your problems,
it's not because your problems
can't be solved.

It's because you have chosen
to hang unto your problems
instead.

If you have done that, that's okay.

Just kindly take credit for it and
don't frustrate the rest of the
world with your baggage.

~

Remarkable success is
exceptionally easy.

Except, of course, for the getting
there.

The reason that you are here is to solve the really big problems.

What is difficult and unpredictable works to our advantage.

If it was any other way, everyone would be doing it.

There would be no exceptional rewards to be gained.

~

On no occasion can you ever pay someone to practice for you.

Well okay, you can, but it won't do you any good.

Do not let them sway you.

If people of few or no major accomplishments in their own lives give you advice about why you should do or not do something, do the opposite.

Nine times out of ten it will be the right thing for you to have done.

~

Choose your companions carefully.

Associate with individuals who play the game of life with a lot more intensity and commitment than you.

When you wind up the smartest person in the room, find another room with much smarter people to hang out with.

If you have always wanted to become a misfit, but have not ever been quite able to make it, then hang around with a bunch of misfits.

If your goal is simply to be average, then hang around with people who are content and grounded in being average.

If you aspire to greatness and making a big difference in this world, however, then hang around with people who themselves aspire to greatness, and are in the process of making a big difference in this world.

You don't need to have everything
be just right.

Nothing immobilizes like the
pursuit of perfection.

Do not wait.

There won't ever be a perfect
time.

Do it badly – but at least do it!

Extraordinary things are attained
by ordinary people who take
the uncertain path.

~

Predict failure in your life and
you will become a psychic with
a pretty good track record.

You are responsible for your life.

Totally!

The important question is:

Will you acknowledge this?

~

Until you take full responsibility for your life, you will experience a lack of freedom and prosperity.

You will call this fate.

The world is much easier to live in when you take 100 percent responsibility for your life.

Taking 100 percent responsibility for your life is your willingness to be the author of all your experiences — including those that you are embarrassed about and that don't make you proud.

~

Most successful, prosperous individuals at one time considered giving up on their dreams and aspirations.

They decided against it, however.

A miracle happens when one of your dreams is attained without your taking what you thought were all the necessary steps to make it happen.

To experience more miracles, take full responsibility for your life.

~

You experience your own world of freedom and prosperity according to your inner vibration.

All the things that truly matter – love, inner peace, true friendship, joy, and making a difference – arise from your cosmic connection with the Universe.

One failure gets you started on
the road to success.

A hundred get you there.

~

There will be days when nothing
goes right.

But all is not lost.

Quite the contrary.

You will learn more from one
day of difficulties than you
will learn from a year of total
pleasure and comfort.

Do not fool yourself about the benefits of working long and hard hours.

The most productive – and smartest – worker is the individual who makes the smallest amount of work go the furthest.

~

At no time economize on the small luxuries of life.

Drinking fine wine and eating chocolate won't solve your problems – but they won't hurt either.

Not happy enough today?

Successful people are happiest when they are making their greatest contribution possible to humanity.

~

Paradise is where you are right now and not where you want to be tomorrow.

Live a little.

Laugh a little.

Love a little.

Happiness will find you in a big way.

You don't have to work hard to attain personal success.

But you have to be committed to some great purpose at least a few hours a day, each and every day.

Commitment is not talking about it.

It's doing what has to be done without looking for excuses why it shouldn't be done.

~

Commitment is the art of being totally devoted to a project or purpose, so much so that you continue even if there are many elements of it that frustrate you to a large degree.

That is what commitment is and not what your school teachers or your parents told you about commitment.

Your life will work precisely to the degree that you keep agreements, those you make with yourself, and those you make with others.

Life is simple when it comes to agreements.

Keep your agreements and your life works.

Don't keep your agreements and your life doesn't work.

Reasons for why you broke your agreements are totally irrelevant.

When you break your agreements and your life doesn't work, don't pray to God to fix what is wrong.

Pray to get your own attention so that you accept that you are the sole reason that your life doesn't work.

What is wrong is that you didn't keep your agreements and you didn't get the results you wanted in your life.

~

Ensure that your actions are always in perfect equilibrium with your goals and dreams.

This will allow you to become a far greater person than you ever imagined yourself to be.

You will encounter many suggestions, blueprints, and schemes on how to achieve prosperity and abundance easily and quickly.

All of them come down to this:

You will end up pursing many things that don't work.

Not for you.

And not for anyone else either.

~

If even a few of all the suggestions, blueprints, and schemes on how to get rich easily and quickly actually worked, wouldn't you already be rich beyond your wildest dreams?

It's futile to dream about what could have been.

Your past is always going to be the way it was, so stop trying to change it.

Live never to be embarrassed by your failures and your past, even if other people are.

Whatever you have done, love yourself for having done it.

~

The past is a nice place to visit.

But you better not make it your home.

Your life is a miracle and does not require you to prove to others that it is so.

~

After you have read all the bestselling books and have heard all the famous gurus speak, what are you going to do for you?

Better still, what are you going to do for the Universe?

The reason you don't get right answers is that you haven't asked the right questions.

~

Suppose God suddenly appeared and asked you, "What are you working on?"

What would you say?

Would you be passionate with your response?

If not, why not?

If you aren't as successful and
   prosperous in life as you would
   like to be, who do you have
   to become before success and
   prosperity flow easily into your
   world?

~

The Universe doesn't reward you
   for the positive and valuable
   things you know.

It rewards you for the positive
   and valuable things you act on.

Taking positive action, even
   small, slow steps, is how you
   send signals to the Universe
   that you are inviting success
   and prosperity into your life.

What would make your heart sing, that would also make you dance in the streets?

If you don't know, who does?

~

Listen to your answers, even when others think that these are answers of a fool.

As long as your answers are your highest truths and coincide with your most cherished dreams, your answers along with creative action will lead you to your destiny where you get to express life in the divine way that the Universe meant you to.

Do you really want to make a big difference in this world and become truly prosperous as a result?

Then go light on the talking – and really heavy on the action instead.

If you can't do that, perhaps you should stop reading this handbook.

Either donate it to a library or give it to someone much more passionate, creative, ambitious, and adventurous.

~

By creative thought, the thing you want is revealed to you.

By much creative action, you receive it.

How many poor souls live all
their lives without finding what
they want and love to do?

Many!

It is your responsibility to ensure
that you are not one of them.

~

Extraordinary prosperity isn't all
that magical.

The road there is, however.

Avoid all the big problems that the Universe sends your way and at no time will you ever become the prosperous and successful individual that you can truly become.

~

If you follow the majority, you will get no further than the majority.

If you make your own path, you are likely to wind up at destinations that the majority only dreams of getting to.

Coming from nothing is an extraordinary place to be coming from because it is only from nothing that you are able to create something extraordinary.

~

Beware your desire for security.

In another twist of irony from the Universe, living with doubt almost always leads to more achievement and prosperity than living with certainty.

Be the unpredictable,
immeasurable, and
indescribable force that
transforms the world instead of
the predictable, measurable, and
describable force that holds the
world back.

~

Your life mission isn't to live the
expected and conventional life
like most people are doing.

Your mission is to express your
love for something unique
that you are doing in the most
adventurous and creative way
you can imagine.

Do enough of what you have always dreamed of doing and there is little time or reason left for feeling unhappy and unfree.

~

Always pursue your goals and dreams with high intention.

Intention is the light and energy that will inspire you to be creative, to be active, and to make a big difference in this world.

When you come from high intention, the Universe will co-create with you.

You will be in a state of awe when it all comes together.

Your question may be:

Where is this incredible spiritual energy called high intention?

Answer:

There is no place around you where there is no high intention if high intention is where you are coming from.

~

How will you know when you are doing what you love to do?

The answer is obvious.

You will know this with so much purity and intensity that no proof will be required.

Trust not what inspires other members of society to choose a career.

Trust what inspires you.

From this decision alone will come over a third of your satisfaction or misery in life.

~

What you choose to do with other people's advice is up to you.

Be sure of one thing, however.

After all is said and done, one of the best reasons for selecting your vocation is that no one told you to.

Only trust the person who tells you to find your highest calling on your own.

Working strictly for money isn't the way to true success in life.

Stop and ponder money in new ways and you will realize many aspects of it are totally absurd.

You will also realize that after basic necessities are provided for, happiness cares little about money.

So, why should you care so much about it?

~

Always reserve enough time in your day to loaf, relax, and think creative thoughts.

This will have much more of a positive effect on your prosperity and personal well-being than several hours of extra work.

Know the moment when to work diligently.

Even more important, know the moment when not to work.

This will not only benefit you immensely, but will also astonish your friends and competitors.

~

When you find yourself on the side of majority, question yourself about what you are doing and why.

It is likely wrong.

You can become a Master at what you want and love to do today.

Simply declare that you are one.

Then make every event in your life a demonstration of your mastery.

~

It's all too easy to forget your previous successes, to think they have been dreams, or small miracles, just one time.

Focus on where your major successes have come from in the past.

These have not been accidents.

Ultimately your success will
be measured not by how hard
you worked, but by what you
accomplished that was a benefit
to humanity.

The purpose of life, therefore,
is to be creatively active, to
be useful, to have made a big
difference that you have lived
at all.

~

Be clear that success doesn't care
how you get there.

Indeed, not only does success
not care how you get there,
it doesn't even care if you get
there at all.

Clearly, you will always have to pay some dues before you attain anything worthwhile.

Don't believe that you have to pay the same dues in time and energy that most other people have to pay, however.

Do not underestimate the essence, the power, and the value of your creativity.

You can climb the ladder of success rung by rung – or you can be creative and skip a number of rungs along the way.

In order that you can experience more success in your world, sometimes you must go backward before you go forward.

Don't ask why.

Some things just work better in practice than they do in theory.

~

You may be reasonable enough to know your limitations.

The important question is:

Are you unreasonable enough to surpass them?

Be careful with taking action on those crazy creative ideas your inner spirit says that you should take action on.

There will be major consequences in your life.

There will be achievement, satisfaction, and prosperity.

And you will sleep happily at night.

The most ambitious destination can be the easiest.

Pursuing your wildest dream does three things:

It gives you flight.

It keeps you young.

It makes you highly creative.

Not to mention, there are other rewards that are just as delightful.

Forget about being "cool."

Cool people are always trying to fit in and seldom make a real difference.

Be unapologetically "uncool."

Make your own path.

Wise people of this world refer to this as being "creatively authentic."

The difference between the "ordinary" and the "extraordinary" has always been – and always will be – the "extra."

How do you intend to put in the "extra" while pursuing your dreams and making an impact in this world?

~

Be ordinary and you will chase success.

Be extraordinary and success will chase you.

Hang around people who empower you to live in truth and love and light.

It's more satisfying to be engaged with one to two like-minded souls working on a small life-changing project that benefits humanity than to be part of a team of ego-trippers working on an amoral project designed only to add dubious growth to an uncaring economy.

~

The more we focus on the acquisition of material possessions as our main reason for living, the more senseless living becomes.

Choose to be a true seeker at heart.

You just may find something that resonates with you, something that you didn't even know you were looking for.

~

You can sit around and climb imaginary mountains because they aren't there.

Or you can commit yourself to action and climb real mountains because they are there.

Which do you think will bring you more satisfaction?

Regardless of how chaotic your world gets, opportunity will spring up out of anywhere and nowhere.

To spot opportunity, follow these three important rituals:

1. Pay attention.
2. Pay attention.
3. Pay attention.

Don't look for perfect opportunities.

There aren't any.

Seize small opportunities, those that are often disguised as common situations, sometimes as impossibilities, and transform them into extraordinary results.

~

So many worlds,

So much to see and do,

So little seen and done by others,

Means many more remarkable things to be seen and done by extraordinary you.

It's easier to speak of dreams than to attain them.

Irrespective of how fantastic your dreams are, they are ten times worse than mediocre when you don't do anything with them.

Sadly, what you don't get around to doing won't ever succeed.

~

Ultimately you will measure your success by how much you had to sacrifice to achieve it.

There is a Spiritual realm that encompasses all Beings.

Embrace your Guardian Angels, who will be out of sight, but always there to assist you.

Make good use of their assistance while creatively pursuing your dreams.

Your success and prosperity will come much easier.

~

Granted, there is little proof for Guardian Angels.

You will be much more inspired, however, to achieve and live your dreams when you trust in Guardian Angels than if you don't trust in them.

You are more than you admit to be.

When you operate with high intention and take creative action, your accomplishments will time and time again come as a surprise to you.

~

Life will always challenge us with things that can be done better.

But don't measure yourself by the best others can do.

Measure yourself by the best that you yourself can do.

If you would like the world to be
happier and more prosperous,
then influence just one
important person to be happier
and more prosperous.

The one important person that
you should influence, by the
way, should be none other than
you.

~

Insights, intuitions, and hunches
will play a big part in your
being extraordinary and making
a big difference in this world.

These are messages from the soul
— even possibly inspirations
from advanced intelligences in
the Universe.

Whatever they are, use them to
your advantage.

Two life courses are available to every one of us:

We can disappear into the main stream.

Or we can be true to ourselves and swim against the current.

One is a form of self-abandonment.

The other is an adventure into new worlds and fascinating dimensions.

~

Learn to actively pursue the alluring rewards of your dreams without compromise or apology.

You will escape into a wondrous adventure that's replete with freedom and prosperity.

To get extraordinary results, you must be different.

To be different, you must be what no other individual but you alone can be.

This is one of the most important things that you must work at – and not ever stop working at.

~

Whatever is important to you, do it well.

Whatever is not that important to you – well, who cares?

Forget about destiny.

You don't need destiny to soar to greater heights.

You need to tune into higher frequencies.

Every soul – including yours – carries the seeds of remarkable accomplishment.

Motivate yourself, inspire yourself, dedicate yourself, and apply yourself.

Because without your best self, the rest of the Universe will be without the wonderful things that you are capable of creating.

~

Live never to be astonished by the accomplishments of others.

Live, instead, to be astonished by your own.

"There's no more opportunity in this world."

Not true!

Everyone, including you, has learned something truly important that someone else needs to learn and is willing to pay for.

How are you going to let them know – and how much are you going to charge?

~

Before you climb over the side of the fence to where the grass appears greener, try watering your side first!

Of three precious resources in life
— time, money, and creativity
— the only one unlimited is your creativity.

Make creativity your number one resource.

The lack of time and money won't be problems anymore.

~

Forget about charm.

You can get by on charm for about five minutes.

After that, you better know something valuable and how to creatively put it to good use for the benefit of humanity.

No other person can force you to take action, even when action is desperately required.

You will take action only when you learn to take responsibility for your life and not count on others to live your life for you.

At this point, you will be in the right place, at the right time, doing the right thing.

~

Aude aliquid dignum.

(Dare something worthy.)

This is your day to do it.

Life's big changes – bad or good –
often come unexpectedly.

Be prepared for either.

Use your creativity to make the
best of all the changes that come
your way;

And most things will turn out just
fine.

~

Your thoughts may be:

"Easy words for you to say.

"Life is much more difficult than
this."

No doubt life is tough.

Even so, you must ask yourself:
"Next to what?"

When money is lost, little is lost;

When time is lost, much more is lost;

When health is lost, practically everything is gone;

And when creative spirit is lost, there is nothing left.

Resist the urge to look for formulas and answers to everything.

Sometimes there are none.

~

There are two principles that govern individual achievement – one general and one definitive.

The general principle is that everyone has the ability to be creative and make a big difference in this world.

The definitive principle is that the vast majority has volunteered to be exempt from the general principle.

Inspiration isn't something that you wait for or something that God gives you.

It's something that's part of you because that's where you are coming from.

~

Within each of us, more than we ever care to admit, resides the power to change our lives.

We can have better health, deeper friendships, everlasting love, more riches, enjoyable work, and greater freedom.

The power lies, not in getting to Heaven, but in using our creativity on Earth.

When first starting out in a new field, ensure that you use your creativity and imagination.

To gain any credibility, you will have to be ten times as creative as the majority – including the veterans and experts.

Luckily, this isn't all that difficult.

~

Creativity is your most valuable asset and your best security.

Thus, ensure that you take care of your mind more than you take care of your possessions.

Unless, of course, you value your possessions more than your mind – then stick with the possessions.

Never be discouraged because others are more privileged or talented than you.

You can always make up in creativity what you lack in good fortune.

Playing the game of life is like playing poker.

Playing three aces badly won't get you as far as playing a terrible hand well.

What most people think is important for creative success is not so significant after all is said and done.

And what most people think is insignificant is vastly more important than most people could ever imagine.

To be more successful, learn to distinguish between the truly unimportant and the truly important.

Eventually you will be considered not only a genius, but a Master as well.

Strive for originality in thought and action.

Be first;

Be different;

And be daring.

Only then will you make a significant impact on this world.

You may even attain greatness.

Be different!

Be really different!

If you are like everyone else, what does the Universe need you here for?

To be really different, you must work at being who no one else but you can be.

~

Don't worry about other people stealing your great idea.

If your idea has the potential to change the world, you will be lucky to get one person just to listen to it.

To have a person steal it – this would be a miracle.

Creativity works in mysterious ways.

Being creative is being naive enough to try something really stupid and find out that it actually works.

~

Be cautious about rejecting your own ideas.

In many completed works of genius by others we often recognize our own previously discarded ideas.

These ideas come back to haunt us with a certain ironic majesty.

Always question what your neighbors say or do or think.

It's unwise to use the conduct of society as a viable precedent for your own life.

Do so and you will be setting yourself up for much disappointment and disenchantment.

What the majority pursues is seldom what will bring happiness, satisfaction, and freedom to any adventurous individual's life.

You should ask yourself whether you want to put in the time and effort to attain extraordinary results.

In spite of the trials and tribulations that the pursuit of success presents, it's still highly popular.

Indeed, there are many people out there who are willing to pay the price of success – and enjoy the prize!

You may want to do the same.

~

The EXTRAORDINARY happens – only if you make it happen.

Mendacity is the fine art of our lying to ourselves and to those around us.

If we get very good at this, we will be able to justify deceit, fraud, false victimhood, freeloading, undeserved income, and a host of other wrongs.

At the extreme, we will even claim these as spiritual pursuits as some people do.

This is not only a form of self-sabotage and a hindrance to our prosperity — but also an insult to the health, well-being, and integrity of the rest of humanity.

Life will continue to be full of surprises regardless of how good we think we are at predicting its consequences.

What we initially see as smiles of good fortune will turn out to be some of the worst things to have happened to us.

And what we initially see as catastrophes will turn out to be some of the best things to have happened to us.

Whatever is important and life-changing to the human soul has to start with difficulty and discomfort.

Make today the day you started the difficult and uncomfortable process that transformed your life.

~

Those who are different change the world.

Those who are ordinary do their best to keep it the way it is.

Pay more attention;

Perceive more;

Listen more;

Think more;

Take more action than the
 average person.

You are now in genius territory.

~

Your talent and creativity are gifts
 that the Universe gave to you.

The inspirational and magical
 things that you do with them
 are the gifts that you give back
 to the Universe.

Time and time again you will meet failure and every time the test will appear:

Can you overcome adversity and continue on to become the happy and successful person that you want to be – the one making a significant difference in this world?

~

The crisis of today is the inspirational story of struggle and accomplishment that you get to tell some time in the near future.

You can have all the knowledge that one can have.

You can be as spiritual as one can be.

You can be as intellectual as one can be.

Without common sense, however, all your efforts to make a real difference will be in vain.

~

Do not delude yourself.

Self-delusion is one of the greatest inventions of the human mind.

It helps many people think that they are Masters of the game of life when, in fact, they are merely impostors.

Anyone can achieve something important.

Contrary to popular belief, the key is not hard work, but finding the right thing to achieve.

~

Beware of false prophets and whimsical gurus whose empty talk is falsely represented as spiritual awakening.

Most are telling you how to make your life work when their own lives are in a big mess.

You cannot fake it until you make it; success is not one motivating thought away; a brand new Porsche cannot be brought into being with a kooky affirmation; a flaky prayer cannot ordain a fabulous career; and whispering hope alone will not manifest superb achievement and render remarkable prosperity.

Only the person of integrity, action, passion, commitment, and goodwill carries in his or her heart the capacity for making a big impact in this world and being rewarded appropriately for it.

Any failure – no matter how unpleasant – isn't a mistake.

Failures are your best teachers.

They are necessary to learn what you must learn, to reach places you have chosen to go.

Ignore these lessons and you will have them reappear again and again.

You will have learned your lesson when your behavior prevents the recurring failure from repeating itself.

You are the source of the miracles in your life.

Miracles go hand in hand with patience and commitment.

Remember not to quit just before the miracle is about to happen.

~

No amount of clever invention will make your excuses a useful tool for explaining the lack of accomplishment and prosperity in your life.

Understand that most people don't spend their time on all things important.

Just because a billion people pursue something doesn't make it worthwhile for you.

On the contrary, it's usually a good sign of the folly of the pursuit.

~

If it lacks integrity, it's not worth pursuing.

Success without integrity – isn't!

Adversity is not what it first appears to be.

It's opportunity looking for some adventurous soul to take advantage of it.

~

Instead of being dismayed, just happily surrender when the world hasn't brought you what you want.

For everything you have been denied, the world has brought you something better.

It's your duty to discover what it is.

You will know when you are
doing something good, right, or
important in this world.

The amount of criticism you
receive will be deafening.

You will acquire more enemies as
well.

~

Being able to ignore your critics
is the ultimate self-care.

Be careful with success.

It's best to stop and ponder what it all means once you acquire it.

Success can also cause misery and dejection.

Don't be surprised when you learn it doesn't bring you all the happiness and peace of mind you thought it would.

~

If your success is not achieved according to your ideals, if your success is impressive to society but does not resonate with your psyche and spirit, then it is not true success at all.

Think often, but not too much.

And not too deeply.

Life is meant to be lived.

It isn't meant to be figured out.

~

When you start doing the right and honorable things that successful people do, you will be liberated from the temptation to theorize that successful people are more privileged and luckier than you.

Be a LEARNER first;

Become a MASTER second;

And remain a STUDENT forever.

The only way to win and be
   successful, sometimes – is just
   to be happy and blown away
   with what you already have
   today.

~

No dark cloud stays around
   forever.

When trouble ensues, hang on.

Live your way through the hazy
   situation the best way you
   know, and in a while, you
   again will be making great
   things happen that help others,
   that make you feel good about
   yourself.

Success leaves clues.

To succeed at anything important, look around you at those souls who are succeeding at the same thing that you want to succeed at.

Then do as they have done.

Simple – isn't it!

~

Be just as enthusiastic about the success of others as you are about your own.

Today's happiness has no past and no future.

It is what it is.

Experience it while you can.

Happiness not enjoyed today is lost forever.

~

To be happy is to have few wants.

To have fewer wants, count your blessings more often.

You don't have to deny yourself
the prosperity and personal
freedom that you would like.

Live in the realm of already
having the prosperity and
personal freedom that you
would like – and pay whatever
price is required to live that
way.

~

Never feel guilty about
experiencing a few comforts in
this world.

Bear in mind, however, that
comfort is a double-edged
sword.

A little will increase health and
happiness.

Too much, and it will destroy
both.

Without problems, you wouldn't have a means to earn a living.

Solving problems also leads to experiences of accomplishment, satisfaction, and abundance.

All told, problems are welcome company for a fulfilling life.

~

To desire prosperity and riches without having earned them honestly through your own creative efforts is to desire the manifestation of a great mistake.

Identify all that is wrong in your life.

Then do what must be done to correct it.

You cannot afford not to.

~

Pursue enough of what you have always wanted to do in your life and there will be no time for you to criticize what other people are doing in theirs.

A little craziness is good for
creative manifestation.

Sometimes the crazier the better.

Take a few risks.

Launch your boat and sail
wherever the wind takes you.

Prosperity favors the brave.

~

Don't be afraid to be outrageous.

Your critics will say nasty things
about you whether you are
outrageous or not.

And your supporters will love
you for it.

What Is Your WOW Factor?

This applies both to the service that you provide to the world and the way you market it.

Make it edgy, make it snappy, and make it punchy.

Even make it raunchy – but make it different!

Real different!

There are two kinds of critics:

Those who know absolutely nothing about your accomplishments.

And those who know a lot.

Don't pay attention to either.

~

Surround yourself with individuals who support and encourage you, who are genuine voices of praise.

Words that inspire the human soul are more precious than money, diamonds, and gold.

Just one great idea can change
your life dramatically.

Look for it.

It's there somewhere.

Experience your uncertain ventures with a good measure of glee.

To be delighted while on the rocky road to success and prosperity is not generally understood by less-adventurous souls.

They will think that you are crazy.

This is the fun part.

~

Don't ever keep a great opportunity waiting.

Three Prosperity Principles for Advanced Souls Playing in the Real World

1. If you want more, make yourself worth more.

2. Be among the best there is in whatever field you are working.

3. Give more than you expect to get in return and eventually you will get more than you expect to get in return.

There's nothing wrong with
working diligently for money
and the many good things money
can buy.

Ensure in your pursuit of money,
however, that you haven't
lost the priceless elements of
happiness that money can't buy.

There are many.

The things that are most precious to the human soul are those that are beyond price.

These include integrity, true friendship, health, achievement, reputation, courage, great character, gratitude, greatness, emotional stability, common sense, self-esteem, creativity, wisdom, spiritual fulfillment, and peace of mind.

These can't be rented, bought, or sold – regardless of how much money you acquire.

Many people will cheer for you when you win.

Who will be there for you when you lose?

A true friend or a confidant will be.

Others won't.

~

Take exceptional care of your reputation.

A great reputation is based on decency, integrity, and excellence.

Remember that a great reputation is much easier kept than won back once it is lost.

Be calm when things don't work
out the way you would like.

Failure is the Universe's way of
ensuring that too much success
doesn't happen all at once.

~

Accept failure and success with
equal grace.

Failure isn't anywhere as tragic
as the mind makes it out to be.

Never expect everything in life to be easy.

If you succeed on the first try, you can be assured that it won't happen again.

Either that, or what you have accomplished is not worth boasting about.

~

If you don't persevere and learn to overcome the biggest of life's challenges, how will you find out how remarkably resourceful you can be?

In the realm of prosperity, luck only favors those adventurous souls who don't rely on luck.

~

Luck is the word most of us give to remarkable achievement by someone less privileged and talented than us.

Believe that remarkable achievement is a matter of luck and you will have a lot of lousy luck come your way.

Accept that remarkable achievement is a matter of personal commitment and well-intentioned action and you will bask in a lot of good luck.

Silence – don't shun it.

Embrace it.

Silence is not only golden.

It's the universal refuge.

That's where you go for calm, peace, self-love, creativity, and energy.

~

Learn to listen intently.

Opportunity often knocks softly.

Competition is good for you in a Divine way.

Your competitors are your spiritual friends.

You learn best and most when you play with those who are much better and more successful than you.

~

When the quest doesn't involve considerable risk, time, and creative energy – and particularly if the doubters of the world aren't laughing at it – it's likely not worth pursuing.

CREATIVITY – that magic serum.

Nothing can make you so lively, bold, and active in the short term and so self-fulfilled and prosperous in the long term.

It's your creativity, your imagination – combined with your go-getting spirit – that will help make you truly prosperous and free.

~

Hard work is simply hard work.

It has nothing to do with the quality of your results and how much you will accomplish in life.

You can't truly start loving others
until you love yourself.

The God source is within you
and not outside you.

Trust it and your love, laughter,
and life will reflect it.

~

Occasionally, you will be
given the chance to be either
intellectual or pleasant.

Leave being intellectual to others.

Nobody on earth forces you to tune into lower frequencies and to live with a lack of abundance.

It's all up to you.

Why frown at your position in life when that is what you have rightfully earned?

If you wanted better, you should have behaved better.

Invite more mentors into your life.

Associate with accomplished individuals – the passionate, the innovative, the risk-takers, the well-intentioned, the doers, and the truly prosperous – those who create value for the Universe and get rewarded handsomely for it.

Allow their spirit to strike a bright light within you, to make your own difference in this world, so that your legacy inspires those adventurous souls who live here after you to do the same.

Live from the perspective that the two most important things that will matter at the end of your stay on Earth are:

1. How big of a difference did you make?

2. Was it a positive, remarkable difference that would make your friends, your family, and anyone else in the Universe feel privileged to have known you?

Look at the world around you.

It may seem like a hard place to live, and a harder place to be happy.

It is neither.

With the right attitude – and your God-given talent – you can make it a Paradise unto itself.

Be careful with your beliefs about what can't be done.

From a human perspective a robin shouldn't be able to find its way over 3,000 miles back to the same nesting place the next spring.

But the robin doesn't know that it shouldn't be able to do this.

So it does.

~

Use your time wisely.

While the misfits and unaccomplished of this world are criticizing and complaining, the adventurous souls of this world are creating wonders and making a difference for the good of humanity.

Your most adventurous and productive ideas will be those that you passionately undertake without being sure they will work.

When your accomplishments eventually motivate other souls to envision more, learn more, become more, and create more, you will know that you are making a big, big difference in this world.

~

A "MASTER" is an amateur who didn't believe in luck.

He or she also didn't quit in the face of adversity.

Do not say yes only to the things that you are comfortable with.

Say yes to challenging opportunities.

Say yes to things that fascinate you.

Say yes to the events that may scare you at first, but in the end will lighten your heart and pacify your soul.

~

When the ship of the adventurous soul hits the reef of criticism, adversity, and failure – it's the criticism, adversity, and failure that are smashed to bits and pieces – and not the adventurous soul.

There is no secret insofar as how to attain prosperity.

The Universe supports and rewards us for taking risks on things that matter to the Universe.

When we remember this, the mysteries about prosperity disappear, and prosperity stands explained.

Prosperity will then manifest itself provided the Universe agrees that we are doing the right things in our lives to deserve this prosperity.

Life is a question and how you live it is your answer.

To achieve your dream of living an uncommon life you must take an uncommon approach to living it.

~

You dedicate your soul to mediocrity when you strive to be just average or a little above average.

This results in more mediocrity or slightly better mediocrity for the planet.

Not a great way to make your mark on this world, is it?

You will have attained true freedom in this world when you can get up in the morning when you want to get up; go to sleep when you want to go to sleep; and in the interval, work and play at the things you want to work and play at – all at your own pace.

The great news is that your imagination and creativity along with inspired action and commitment can help you attain this freedom.

Any thought system that seems totally reasonable and valuable to the common mind — but doesn't elevate the inner spirit to achieving results of self-sufficiency, love, kindness, happiness, and prosperity — is uninteresting and immaterial to the impassioned adventurous soul.

~

Secrecy can be magical as you pursue your dreams.

Envelope your actions in a veil of mystery that commands respect from others.

You will find that it's truly satisfying to let others wonder and watch while you create results that astound the world.

One day a great idea that can dramatically change your life will present itself.

So simple, yet so genius.

It will be there hiding in plain sight in front of you.

Will you do anything with it?

~

What will you do if your crazy creative idea actually works?

Can you handle the success and prosperity that it will bring you?

Did you know that highly-spirited successful souls are thankful for the critics, the faultfinders, and the nit-pickers of this world for constantly trying to put them down?

This gives these highly-spirited souls the inspiration to learn how to fly, to soar even higher with their dreams, to make an even bigger contribution to this world, and to be rewarded even more handsomely with the finer things of life that the Universe has to offer.

~

Selling out to be popular in society is selling yourself short.

Anything mainstream is not the stream that ambitious creative people want to be in.

Are your words of advice to others congruent with how you live your life?

If not, something is suspect:

Either your advice.

Or the way you live your life!

~

What important truth are you willing to stand up for, and in the eyes of others, to be unreasonable about?

Better to do work that's worth doing.

Show the world that you are
  here to make a big difference.

Transform your important
  thoughts and dreams into
  inspired action.

Otherwise you're all talk.

~

Ensure not to take half measures
  on what is important to you.

The middle way only leads to
  insufficiency and shortfalls.

Many regrets, too.

While effort is certainly important for success in any field, effort by itself will get us nowhere.

Effort must be directed in the right places.

Otherwise effort will show little in the way of positive results and may even get us to the wrong places.

~

Look to make the smallest move that gives you the biggest gain.

That's what genius is all about.

It's also known as working smart instead of working hard.

Keep focused and innovative.

Occupy yourself one project at a time.

Make sure that it is the right project.

Success isn't a game won by whoever does the most.

It's won by whoever knows the right important thing to pursue.

~

It takes an astute person to recognize the inconsequential.

It takes an even more astute person to ignore it.

Do you wish for all the material possessions that any human being can possibly acquire?

This is not very much to long for.

What about the things that truly matter?

~

Pray not for material things.

Pray instead for inspiration, motivation, enthusiasm, courage, creativity, health, and wisdom.

You cannot afford to play roulette with your reputation.

Always operate with sterling excellence, preserving your good name with correctness and integrity.

Hold yourself firmly to the highest standards that you would place on any Messiah.

~

Regardless how much you want to change the world, be gentle with Earth and all its magnificence.

If only one impassioned adventurous soul works diligently to create a world that he or she believes in – one that is full of love and joy and decency and creativity and integrity and freedom and opportunity and self-sufficiency and excellence and truth and justice – and if he or she fails to come close in manifesting this kind of visionary world before he or she passes away to a different dimension, it's not this one impassioned adventurous soul who is crazy.

It's the rest of humanity.

Always be true to yourself.

Do not blindly believe what brings happiness, even what is said in this handbook.

Find out for yourself what brings joy and contentment to your world.

Your inner voice will tell you what will bring you peace of mind.

Listen to it carefully.

A dramatically different tomorrow starts with a dramatically different you today.

Inspiration manifests magic.

And prosperity, too!

Today can be the day you start making that difference.

Or tomorrow.

Don't put it off too long, however.

It's up to you.

Life is short and time runs out quickly.

~

Death often comes at a bad time.

Prosperous

        and

                Free.

You can't be one − without the other.

No one can compel you to become prosperous and free.

You will become prosperous and free when you want to.

Be prepared for surprises.

For instance, there will be some delightful work involved.

Taking 100 percent responsibility for our lives is the one thing that most of us dread more than anything else.

Yet it is the one factor in the world that will distinguish any one of us from the majority, the one element that gives us wings of flight and ascends us to the realm of extraordinary achievement and remarkable prosperity.

~

Taking responsibility for your life is about being your own hero, becoming truly prosperous and free, without the sanction of society, government, friends, family, or any other forces that have no idea what your life is supposed to be all about.

Attaining freedom in a generally unfree world is not well understood by less adventurous souls.

You experience your personal world – free or unfree – according to what you focus on and what you create for yourself.

Hitch your dreams to a star and not to a wagon.

Make your dreams real.

Your dreams are the path between the person you are today and the person you want to be tomorrow.

Whatever you do, don't let go of these dreams.

A dream without a plan kindled by your inspired action is just a wish that the Universe has little interest in supporting.

Inspired action leads to transcendent wonder and smiles of good fortune.

That is to say, supreme blessings of prosperity from the Universe are the result of supreme impassioned inputs from you.

Your creativity allows an idea to manifest itself.

Your actions allow the idea to become real and start a life of its own.

Your commitment to the idea allows it to eventually come to its natural perfect end as an important benefit to both you and the rest of humanity.

Always do your best to make a big difference in this world.

When you live your best, and always do your best, the results that you attain are, in fact, perfect.

Whatever the results – they couldn't have come out any better.

While little guidance was provided to you about your purpose when you were born, the choices that you will have made throughout your life will be measured by this view:

If your stay here on Earth leaves a legacy that inspires other souls to follow their dreams and become more than they ever imagined, your mission will have been fulfilled.

If you are truly committed to success, aren't you already there?

Serving people with light, love, and laughter — while making a positive difference in this world — is about as successful as you can become.

Don't ever grow up.

Be forever young in spirit.

Spend your entire life in the most inspirational, adventurous, and creative way possible.

About the Author

Ernie J. Zelinski is an international best-selling author, prosperity life coach, innovator, speaker, and unconventional career expert. Ernie has helped thousands of individuals from all walks of life in their major career transitions and retirement planning through his life-changing books.

Ernie's fifteen creative works — published in twenty-two languages in twenty-nine countries — have sold over 975,000 copies worldwide. His two international bestsellers *The Joy of Not Working* and *How to Retire Happy, Wild, and Free* have been featured in major international media such as *The Wall Street Journal* and have sold a total of over 650,000 copies.

Ernie speaks on the topics of retirement, leisure, and creativity. He recently made keynote speeches about *The Joy of Not Working* to over 2,000 executives and scholars at the National Turkish Congress on Quality in Istanbul and to 1,200 career experts at the National Career Development Association convention in Orlando, FL.